THE ULTIMATE AVATAR THE LAST AIRBENDER COOKBOOK

The Beginners Recipes and Meals Guide

Craig Josh
Copyright@2023

TABLE OF CONTENT

CHAPTER 1

INTRODUCTION

The Avatar: The Last Airbender Cookbook offers readers a gastronomic journey that vividly captures the rich and multifaceted universe of the popular animated series, presenting an assortment of delectable recipes. This cookbook provides fans and individuals interested in food with a chance to explore the diverse culinary traditions of the four nations portrayed in the show:

Throughout history, food has consistently held a prominent position within human culture, fulfilling various functions such as providing nourishment, facilitating communal festivities, and contributing to the formation of individual and collective identities. Within the realm of Avatar, a universe characterized by the harmonious fusion of elemental manipulation and spiritual interconnectedness, the significance of sustenance emerges as a pivotal narrative element, effectively mirroring the distinct societal practices, cultural heritage, and ethical principles upheld by each respective nation. The culinary offerings of the Avatar universe encompass a diverse range of gastronomic experiences, spanning from the piquant Fire Nation delicacies to the nourishing stews of the Water Tribe, the earthy cuisine of the Earth Kingdom, and the ethereal and delicate treats of the Air Nomads. These delectable creations serve as a conduit for exploring the rich tapestry of cultural heritage and the profound influence of the elemental forces within this fictional realm.

Food in the series serves a dual purpose, functioning not only as a means of sustenance but also as a symbolic representation of the characters' personal growth and the state of their nations, either fostering unity or highlighting discord. The medium in question functions as a channel for narrative, emphasizing the interrelationships among characters, their respective cultural backgrounds, and the broader context of their shared environment. The Avatar: The Last Airbender Cookbook demonstrates a profound appreciation for the intricate storytelling of the series by effectively encapsulating the essence of its food-focused universe. It extends an invitation to readers, encouraging them to embark on a personal culinary journey that allows for a firsthand encounter with this captivating world.

The Fire Nation, known for its passionate disposition and robust capabilities, introduces assertive and piquant tastes to the culinary repertoire. The recipes presented here exemplify the bold and daring essence of Fire Nation cuisine, ranging from the flavorful Fire Nation Spicy Ramen, characterized by its fragrant broth and vibrant toppings, to the fiery Fire Flakes that offer a powerful and intense experience.

On the other hand, the culinary practices of the Water Tribe exemplify the tenacity and ingenuity of its inhabitants. The dietary preferences of the individuals have been influenced by the severe winter conditions and frozen terrains, resulting in a focus on substantial and nutritious culinary choices. One notable recipe within this compilation is the Water Tribe Seafood Stew, which presents itself as a comforting and flavorful culinary creation that harmoniously merges the abundant offerings of the ocean with the comforting ambiance of a domestic setting.

The Earth Kingdom, being the largest and most culturally heterogeneous nation, presents a diverse array of culinary traditions. One of the notable culinary offerings is the Earth Kingdom Cabbage Rolls, which serve as a tribute to the nation's profound affiliation with the earth and its bountiful agricultural yields. These cabbage rolls, characterized by their diverse assortment of ingredients and accompanied by zesty sauces, serve as a prime example of the Earth Kingdom's commitment to nourishing and gratifying gastronomy.

The Air Nomads, renowned for their profound spirituality and profound affinity with the air element, possess a culinary tradition that prioritizes qualities of delicacy and minimalism. The Air Nomad Fruit Pies encapsulate the fundamental aspects of their nomadic way of life, exhibiting a refined pastry shell and a delectable fruit filling that serves as a tribute to the revered natural environment. The pies serve as a symbol of the Air Nomads' harmonious coexistence and their gratitude towards the abundant offerings of the natural world.

In addition to the four nations, the Avatar universe encompasses the Spirit World, a realm characterized by its mystical qualities and ethereal aesthetics. The Spirit World Herbal Tea draws inspiration from the earthly realm, amalgamating a meticulously curated assortment of botanicals to produce a calming and contemplative infusion. This recipe promotes an exploration of the spiritual dimension of food and encourages individuals to embrace the serene qualities associated with the Spirit World.

The Avatar: The Last Airbender Cookbook provides an enriching gastronomic encounter while simultaneously serving as a conduit for comprehending the profound interrelationships among cuisine, societal customs, and individuality. By engaging in the practice of preparing and exchanging these culinary formulas, individuals are able to embark on a personal and transformative expedition, acquiring profound understanding of the varied customs and ideologies that influence the realm of Avatar.

This cookbook extends an invitation to individuals, regardless of their level of enthusiasm for the series, to partake in the culinary exploration of new and stimulating flavors. By engaging in the act of cooking, readers are encouraged to commemorate the essence of Avatar and its associated sentiments. Please join us as we embark on a gastronomic journey through the four nations, delving into the flavors, fragrances, and narratives that render this universe so captivating. Prepare yourself by donning an apron, honing your culinary tools, and embarking on a gastronomic journey to the captivating realm of Avatar, where its exquisite cuisine awaits.

CHAPTER 2

AVATAR THE LAST AIRBENDER COOKBOOK

Recipe 1: Fire Nation Spicy Ramen

The Fire Nation is widely recognized for its distinctive culinary traditions, characterized by a vibrant cultural heritage and a penchant for bold and spicy flavors. The Fire Nation Spicy Ramen is regarded as a notable culinary creation originating from this particular country. This delectable recipe combines a variety of fragrant flavors, substantial noodles, and intense spices to produce a bowl of piping hot ramen that will tantalize your taste buds and transport you to the core of the Fire Nation.

Ingredients

Ingredients and Measurements: In order to replicate the genuine Fire Nation Spicy

Ramen, it is necessary to assemble the subsequent ingredients:

The recipe calls for 8 ounces of ramen noodles, 4 cups of vegetable or chicken broth, and 2 tablespoons of soy sauce.

- Two tablespoons of gochujang, a traditional Korean chili paste,
- One tablespoon of sriracha sauce should be used, with the option to adjust the quantity according to personal preference for spiciness.

The recipe calls for the inclusion of the following ingredients: one tablespoon of sesame oil, one tablespoon of grated ginger, and four cloves of minced garlic.

The ingredients required for this recipe include one small onion that has been thinly sliced, one medium carrot that has been julienned, and one red bell pepper that has been thinly sliced.

- One cup of sliced mushrooms, such as shiitake or cremini, is required.

- Two green onions, sliced into thin pieces - Two boiled eggs, cut in half

- The optional toppings that can be added to the dish include sliced red chili peppers, bean sprouts, cilantro, and sesame seeds.

Procedures

Step-by-Step To commence, initiate the process by meticulously following the guidelines provided on the packaging to properly prepare the ramen noodles. The pasta should be cooked until it reaches the desired level of firmness known as "al dente." Subsequently, it should be drained and set aside.

2. The sesame oil is heated in a large pot over medium heat. Incorporate the minced garlic and grated ginger into the mixture,

and proceed to sauté for approximately one minute until an aromatic scent is emitted.

Subsequently, incorporate the sliced onion, julienned carrot, red bell pepper, and sliced mushrooms into the cooking vessel. The vegetables should be stir-fried for an estimated duration of 3 to 4 minutes, or until they exhibit signs of initial softening.

In a diminutive container, combine the soy sauce, gochujang, sriracha sauce, and vegetable or chicken broth using a whisk. Transfer the mixture into the cooking vessel containing the vegetables and proceed to heat it until it reaches its boiling point.

The heat should be decreased to a low setting, and the broth should be allowed to simmer for approximately 10 to 15 minutes, facilitating the harmonization of flavors.

During the simmering process of the broth, it is recommended to prepare the optional toppings. To enhance the flavor profile, one may opt to finely cut red chili peppers, cleanse and scald bean sprouts, finely dice fresh cilantro, and lightly toast sesame seeds.

To facilitate the distribution of the cooked ramen noodles, it is recommended to partition them into individual serving bowls. Carefully pour the heated and flavorful broth onto the noodles, ensuring that the vegetables are evenly dispersed.

To enhance the presentation, adorn the bowls with thinly sliced green onions and delicately position a halved boiled egg atop each portion.

If preferred, one may include supplementary toppings such as thinly sliced red chili peppers, blanched bean sprouts, fresh cilantro, or toasted sesame seeds.

Optimal consumption of Fire Nation Spicy Ramen is achieved when the dish is served at a high temperature. Promptly serve the dish, thereby enabling the fragrance to captivate one's sensory perceptions. The combination of a piquant broth, resilient noodles, and crunchy vegetables results in a cohesive amalgamation of diverse textures and flavors. The inclusion of optional toppings provides additional dimensions of spiciness, texture, and vibrancy to the culinary preparation.

To fully immerse oneself in the culinary traditions of the Fire Nation, it is advisable to complement the ramen dish with Fire Flakes, a widely consumed snack renowned within the Fire Nation. These chips, which possess a crispy texture and a spicy flavor, can be consumed independently or crushed and sprinkled atop ramen to provide an additional element of spiciness.

In order to achieve a harmonious flavor profile, it is recommended to complement the heat of the ramen by serving it in conjunction with a refreshing cucumber salad or pickled vegetables. The invigorating and acidic flavors will offer a pleasant juxtaposition to the piquancy of the dish.

The Fire Nation Spicy Ramen exemplifies the culinary traditions of the Fire Nation, characterized by its robust taste profiles and fervent culinary style. This recipe encourages individuals to embrace their adventurous nature and embark on a culinary exploration that honors the vibrant culture of the Fire Nation. The following instructions entail the gathering of necessary ingredients, the preparation of one's palate, and the anticipation of indulging in a bowl of piping hot Fire Nation Spicy Ramen, an experience that will evoke a sense of immersion within the Avatar universe.

Recipe 2: Water Tribe Seafood Stew
The Water Tribe, renowned for its tenacity and profound affinity with the ocean, possesses a culinary heritage centered on robust and nourishing cuisine. The Seafood

Stew is considered one of the culinary gems within the Water Tribe's gastronomic repertoire, renowned for its rich and satisfying taste. This culinary preparation combines a variety of recently caught marine creatures, fragrant plant-based ingredients, and flavorful seasonings to produce a decadent and gratifying soup that acknowledges the abundance of the sea and the comfort of one's dwelling.

Ingredients

Ingredients and Measurements: In order to replicate the genuine Water Tribe Seafood Stew, it is necessary to assemble the subsequent ingredients:
- One pound of assorted seafood, including shrimp, mussels, clams, and white fish fillets. - Two tablespoons of olive oil. - One large onion, finely diced. - Three cloves of

garlic, minced. - Two medium-sized carrots, diced.

Two stalks of celery, finely chopped.

One red bell pepper, finely chopped.

- One can of diced tomatoes, measuring 14 ounces.

- Four cups of fish or seafood broth - One teaspoon of dried thyme - One teaspoon of paprika

- One bay leaf - Salt and pepper, adjusted according to personal preference - Finely chopped fresh parsley, utilized as a garnish

Procedures

Step-by-Step To commence, begin the process by preparing the seafood. The shrimp should be cleaned and deveined, while the mussels and clams should be scrubbed. Additionally, the white fish fillets should be cut into bite-sized pieces. Place the seafood in a separate location.

2. In a capacious vessel or Dutch oven, commence the heating process of the olive oil on a medium heat setting. Incorporate the diced onion and minced garlic into the mixture, and proceed to sauté for approximately 3-4 minutes until they emit a pleasant aroma and achieve a translucent appearance.

Next, incorporate the finely chopped carrots, celery, and red bell pepper into the cooking vessel. Continue to cook the mixture, intermittently stirring, for an additional duration of 5 minutes until the vegetables begin to exhibit signs of tenderness.

Next, add the diced tomatoes along with their juices and the fish or seafood broth. Incorporate the dried thyme, paprika, bay leaf, salt, and pepper into the mixture. Heat the mixture until it reaches a simmering point.

After the stew has reached a simmering state, it is advised to cautiously incorporate the seafood into the pot. Carefully agitate the mixture in order to fully immerse the seafood within the broth. Proceed by placing a lid on the pot, allowing the stew to simmer for approximately 8-10 minutes. This duration is necessary to ensure that the seafood is thoroughly cooked and that the mussels and clams have opened.

After the seafood has been cooked, it is advisable to remove the pot from the heat source. Dispose of any mussels or clams that have failed to open.

The Water Tribe Seafood Stew should be served hot, with the stew being carefully ladled into individual bowls and garnished with a generous amount of freshly chopped parsley. The stew is complemented by the addition of crusty bread or steamed rice.

Serving Recommendations: The Water Tribe Seafood Stew is a nourishing and gratifying culinary preparation that can be savored either as a standalone dish or in combination with complementary accompaniments to enhance the overall dining experience.

The stew should be accompanied by a serving of crusty bread, which will effectively absorb the rich broth. The inclusion of slices of freshly baked bread or a warm baguette can contribute a pleasant crispness and tactile quality to every mouthful.

To enhance the meal's substantiality, it is advisable to serve the stew atop a foundation of steamed rice. The rice will undergo absorption of the flavorful broth, resulting in a delectable and comforting amalgamation.

In order to introduce a revitalizing component to the dining experience, it is recommended to accompany the main dish with a vibrant green salad. The incorporation of a diverse range of hues and the incorporation of a zesty vinaigrette in a composite green salad can effectively enhance the opulence of the seafood stew.

The Water Tribe Seafood Stew exemplifies the culinary heritage of the Water Tribe, showcasing an array of pristine seafood and wholesome components. This recipe encourages individuals to embrace the enduring qualities and interconnection with the ocean that characterize the cultural heritage of the Water Tribe. In order to commence the culinary process, it is necessary to assemble the requisite components, ready oneself for the gustatory experience, and anticipate the consumption of a nourishing and delectable Seafood Stew inspired by the Water Tribe. This dish possesses the ability to transport individuals to the core of the Avatar universe, evoking a sense of nostalgia for the concepts of home, community, and the bountiful offerings of the sea.

Recipe 3: Earth Kingdom Cabbage Rolls

The Earth Kingdom, which is the largest and most diverse nation within the Avatar universe, possesses a notable culinary heritage. One of the highly regarded culinary creations is the Earth Kingdom Cabbage Rolls. These delectable rolls exemplify the Earth Kingdom's profound bond with the land and their profound admiration for nourishing and comforting gastronomy. These rolls, consisting of a delectable blend of ingredients encased in delicate cabbage leaves, serve as a delightful embodiment of the culinary customs prevalent in the Earth Kingdom.

Ingredients

Ingredients and Measurements: In order to replicate the traditional Earth Kingdom Cabbage Rolls, it is necessary to assemble the subsequent ingredients:

- One sizable cabbage head - One pound of ground meat, which may consist of beef, pork, or a blend of both.

The recipe calls for the following ingredients: one cup of cooked rice, one small onion that has been finely chopped, two cloves of garlic that have been minced, one carrot that has been grated, one zucchini that has been grated, one teaspoon of dried thyme, and one teaspoon of paprika.

- Adjust the amount of salt and pepper according to personal preference. - Incorporate one can of crushed tomatoes, measuring 14 ounces. - Integrate one cup of vegetable or beef broth. - Employ freshly chopped parsley as a garnish.

Procedures

The first step involves the preparation of the cabbage. Eliminate any externally impaired outer leaves from the cabbage head. Heat a substantial quantity of water until it reaches its boiling point, then cautiously submerge the intact cabbage head into the pot. The cooking process should be continued for approximately 5 to 7 minutes, or until the outer leaves reach a state of tenderness and flexibility. Extract the cabbage from the cooking vessel and allow it to cool to a moderate temperature.

2. During the cooling process of the cabbage, proceed with the preparation of the filling. In a voluminous mixing vessel, amalgamate the pulverized meat, cooked rice, diced onion, minced garlic, grated carrot, grated zucchini, desiccated thyme, paprika, salt, and pepper. Combine the ingredients thoroughly until a homogeneous mixture is achieved.

The oven should be preheated to a temperature of 375°F (190°C). Prepare a baking dish that has the capacity to accommodate the cabbage rolls in a singular layer.

After the cabbage has sufficiently cooled, proceed with caution to remove the individual leaves, ensuring their preservation and minimizing any damage. To facilitate the rolling process, it is advisable to remove the central rib of each leaf, which is relatively thick.

To initiate the process, acquire a cabbage leaf and proceed to position a spoonful of the filling mixture in close proximity to the lowermost section, specifically the stem end, of the leaf. Proceed by folding the edges of the leaf inwards, encompassing the filling, and subsequently tightly rolling it, akin to the process of rolling a burrito. Proceed by repeating the aforementioned process with the remaining cabbage leaves and filling.

The rolled cabbage leaves should be placed in the prepared baking dish with the seam-side facing downwards, ensuring that they are arranged in a single layer.

In a distinct container, combine the crushed tomatoes with either vegetable or beef broth. Carefully pour the mixture over the cabbage rolls, ensuring that they are partially immersed in the liquid.

To initiate the cooking process, proceed by enveloping the baking dish with a layer of aluminum foil, subsequently positioning it within the oven that has been preheated. The recommended baking time for the cabbage rolls is approximately 45-50 minutes, or until they are fully cooked and the flavors have harmonized.

After the completion of the cooking process for the cabbage rolls, proceed to carefully remove the foil covering and proceed to enhance their visual appeal by adorning them with a generous amount of freshly chopped parsley. Present the rolls in a heated manner, ensuring that a portion of the tomato broth is carefully poured over each one.

Serving Recommendations: The Earth Kingdom Cabbage Rolls can be savored either on their own or in combination with compatible side dishes.

To create a comprehensive meal inspired by the Earth Kingdom, it is recommended to accompany the cabbage rolls with a serving of roasted root vegetables. When infused with a blend of aromatic herbs and spices, the roasted medley of potatoes, carrots, and parsnips can offer a gratifying and rustic juxtaposition to the accompanying rolls.

To enhance the culinary experience, it is recommended to include a cucumber and yogurt salad as a complementary accompaniment to the cabbage rolls, providing a refreshing and zesty flavor profile. To prepare this dish, one must combine thinly sliced cucumbers with Greek yogurt, lemon juice, and an assortment of fresh herbs, such as dill or mint.

To enhance the meal's substantiality, it is recommended to serve the cabbage rolls alongside a side dish of mashed potatoes.

The velvety and rich consistency of the mashed potatoes serves as a comforting foundation that harmonizes with the robust flavors of the rolls.

The Earth Kingdom Cabbage Rolls exemplify the Earth Kingdom's culinary customs, demonstrating their affiliation with the natural environment and admiration for nourishing and substantial cuisine. This recipe encourages individuals to delve into the varied flavors and textures of the Earth Kingdom by means of the soothing and tender cabbage leaves. In order to commence the culinary process, it is necessary to assemble the required ingredients, ready oneself for the gustatory experience, and anticipate the consumption of a generous portion of Earth Kingdom Cabbage Rolls. This particular dish possesses the ability to transport individuals to the core of the Avatar universe, evoking a sense of nostalgia for the opulent and diverse customs of this extraordinary nation.

Recipe 4: Air Nomad Fruit Pies

The Air Nomads, renowned for their profound spiritual affinity and serene coexistence, possess a culinary tradition that mirrors their ethereal and unpretentious manner of living. Included in their assortment of palatable delicacies are the Air Nomad Fruit Pies. These delectable pastries commemorate the abundance of the natural world and the Air Nomads' profound reverence for the environment. Characterized by a delicate outer layer and a delectable filling comprised of various fruits, these fruit pies serve as a flawless representation of the Air Nomad philosophy and offer a delightful indulgence suitable for any event or circumstance.

Ingredients

Ingredients and Measurements: In order to replicate the genuine Air Nomad Fruit Pies, it is necessary to assemble the subsequent ingredients:

To prepare the pie crust:

The recipe calls for 2 ½ cups of all-purpose flour and 2 tablespoons of granulated sugar. - A quantity of salt measuring half a teaspoon - One cup of butter that is unsalted, chilled, and divided into small cubes.

Approximately 6 to 8 tablespoons of ice.Cold water is a liquid with a low temperature.

The fruit filling consists of 4 cups of fresh fruit, which may include berries, peaches, or apples. The fruit should be properly washed, peeled, and sliced.

- A quantity of granulated sugar equivalent to half a cup, to be adjusted based on the desired level of sweetness of the fruit. The recipe calls for 2 tablespoons of cornstarch and 1 tablespoon of lemon juice.

- One teaspoon of vanilla extract is recommended for use. - Additionally, one teaspoon of ground cinnamon may be added, although this is optional.

The egg wash, consisting of one beaten egg combined with one tablespoon of milk, is utilized.

Procedures

Step-by-Step To commence, initiate the process by preparing the pie crust. The flour, sugar, and salt should be combined in a large mixing bowl. Incorporate the chilled butter cubes into the flour mixture, employing either a pastry cutter or manual manipulation with your fingers, until the resulting texture resembles coarse crumbs.

In a gradual manner, incorporate the ice-cold water into the mixture, adding one tablespoon at a time. Utilize a fork to combine the ingredients until the dough reaches a cohesive state.
After the dough has coalesced into a cohesive mass, proceed to divide it evenly into two portions. Proceed to mold each portion into a flat, circular shape, and subsequently enclose them individually in a layer of plastic wrap.

It is recommended to place the dough in a refrigerated environment for a minimum duration of one hour.

During the period of dough refrigeration, proceed with the preparation of the fruit filling. In an independent container, amalgamate the recently harvested fruit, granulated sugar, cornstarch, lemon juice, vanilla extract, and ground cinnamon (if preferred). Carefully and delicately mix the ingredients together until the fruit is evenly covered with the sugar and cornstarch blend. Allow the filling to rest for approximately 15 to 20 minutes in order to facilitate the harmonization of flavors.

The oven should be preheated to a temperature of 375°F (190°C).

To begin, select a disk of the refrigerated pie dough and proceed to roll it out on a surface lightly dusted with flour, ensuring that it is sized appropriately to fit the dimensions of your pie dish. With caution, transfer the flattened dough to the pie dish and firmly press it against the bottom and sides. Remove any excess dough that extends beyond the edges.

To commence, carefully transfer the fruit filling into the pie crust, ensuring an even distribution.

To proceed, extend the second disk of dough in order to form the upper crust. There are two options available for the placement of the dough in relation to the fruit filling. The first option involves placing the entire rolled-out dough on top of the filling, while the second option entails cutting the dough into strips and weaving them in a lattice design over the filling.

8. After positioning the upper crust, proceed to crimp the periphery of the pie

by employing either manual finger pressure or a utensil such as a fork, thereby effectuating the fusion of the two crust layers. Create several minor incisions on the upper crust to facilitate the release of steam while the baking process is underway.

To achieve a golden and glossy finish on the pie, it is recommended to apply an egg wash to the top crust.

10. Position the pie onto a baking sheet (to capture any potential liquid overflow) and proceed to bake it within the preheated oven for an estimated duration of 45-50 minutes, or until the crust achieves a desirable golden brown hue and the fruit filling exhibits bubbling activity.

After the pie has finished baking, it should be taken out of the oven and allowed to cool on a wire rack prior to being served. This process will enable the fruit filling to solidify.

Optimal consumption of Air Nomad Fruit Pies is achieved when they are heated or consumed at ambient temperature. These items have the potential to be enjoyed individually or in conjunction with complementary additions, thereby augmenting the overall sensory encounter.

The addition of a scoop of vanilla ice cream or a dollop of freshly whipped cream can serve as an ideal complement to the warm fruit pie. The juxtaposition of the cool and creamy components offers a pleasurable juxtaposition to the rich and velvety crust and the fruity filling.

To enhance the presentation, it is recommended to garnish the pie with a light dusting of powdered sugar or cinnamon sugar immediately prior to serving. This will introduce a delicate level of sweetness and enhance the aesthetic appeal.

In order to enhance the visual appeal of the presentation, it is advisable to adorn each individual slice with a small sprig of freshly-picked mint or a delicate sprinkling of cocoa powder. The inclusion of these minute particulars has the potential to enhance the aesthetic appeal and allure of the dessert.

Air Nomad Fruit Pies exemplify the fundamental principles of the Air Nomad lifestyle, characterized by its emphasis on simplicity and reverence for the natural world. Characterized by a delicate outer layer and a delectable filling comprised of succulent fruits, these pies beckon individuals to indulge in the inherent tastes and appreciate the pleasure derived from uncomplicated culinary experiences. The following instructions will guide you in assembling the necessary ingredients, preparing your palate, and anticipating the enjoyment of a portion of Air Nomad Fruit Pie. This culinary creation will evoke a sense of immersion in the Avatar universe, evoking an appreciation for the tranquility and splendor inherent in life's most minute occurrences.

Recipe 5: Spirit World Herbal Tea

Within the metaphysical domain known as the Spirit World, a realm characterized by the convergence of mysticism and spirituality, the denizens possess a deep-seated affinity for the natural world and its inherent therapeutic attributes. The Spirit World Herbal Tea is a beverage that offers a calming and contemplative experience, drawing inspiration from the enigmatic realm of mysticism. By skillfully amalgamating a meticulously chosen assortment of botanical elements, this infusion not only stimulates gustatory sensations but also elicits a profound state of serenity and equilibrium. We invite you to accompany us on a venture to craft a captivating concoction that will transport you to a tranquil domain inhabited by ethereal beings.

Ingredients and Measurements: In order to replicate the genuine Spirit World Herbal Tea, it is necessary to assemble the subsequent ingredients:

- One tablespoon of dried chamomile flowers
- One tablespoon of dried lavender blossoms

The ingredients required for this preparation are as follows: one tablespoon of dried lemon balm leaves, one tablespoon of dried peppermint leaves, one tablespoon of dried hibiscus petals, one teaspoon of dried rose petals, and four cups of water.

- Honey or a preferred sweetener may be added as an optional ingredient.

Step-by-Step Procedure: 1. In a vessel such as a teapot or a container that can withstand heat, amalgamate the dried chamomile flowers, lavender blossoms, lemon balm leaves, peppermint leaves, hibiscus petals, and rose petals. Carefully agitate the herbs in order to achieve a thorough mixture.

To commence the process, heat a kettle or saucepan and bring 4 cups of water to its boiling point.

3. Subsequent to the attainment of a vigorous boiling state, exercise caution while transferring the water onto the amalgamation of herbs within the teapot or any container that is resistant to heat.

4. Proceed by placing a lid or plate over the teapot or container, allowing the herbs to infuse in the heated water for approximately 5 to 7 minutes. This process facilitates the infusion of the herbs' flavors and aromas into the water.

Upon completion of the designated steeping duration, proceed to strain the tea into either separate cups or a communal serving vessel, while simultaneously disposing of the utilized herbal components.

If preferred, the tea can be sweetened with honey or the sweetener of one's choice. Gently agitate the mixture until the sweetener has completely dissolved.

The Spirit World Herbal Tea can be savored in its hot form, offering a serene and invigorating experience.

Optional Additions and Variations: The customization of the Spirit World Herbal Tea allows for tailoring the beverage to individual preferences. The following are several optional additions and variations that can be explored:

To enhance the flavor profile of your tea, consider incorporating a citrus twist by including a slice of freshly cut lemon or a small quantity of lemon juice in each cup. This addition will impart a refreshing and invigorating citrus note to your beverage. To enhance the flavor profile with a spicy and invigorating element, it is recommended to grate a small portion of fresh ginger and steep it together with the herbs.

- Incorporate a refreshing minty essence into the tea by crushing a small quantity of fresh mint leaves and infusing them during the steeping phase, thereby imparting a cool and invigorating undertone.

- Floral Infusion: Conduct an experimental investigation involving the incorporation of alternative dried flowers, such as chamomile, jasmine, or calendula, in order to introduce diverse floral characteristics to the tea.

One possible variation for preparing iced tea involves allowing the steeped tea to cool down to the ambient room temperature before transferring it to the refrigerator for the purpose of chilling. To provide a revitalizing iced tea alternative, it is recommended to serve the Spirit World Herbal Tea over ice.

Serving Recommendations and Tea Etiquette: For optimal enjoyment of the Spirit World Herbal Tea, it is advisable to partake in a tranquil and serene setting that facilitates a complete immersion in its soothing attributes. Please take into account the following recommendations in order to optimize your tea consumption experience:

To establish a serene atmosphere, locate a secluded and comfortable area in which you may unwind and savor the tea undisturbed.

- Select a teacup or mug that elicits feelings of joy and enhances the visual appeal of the act of consuming tea.

It is recommended to pause briefly in order to acknowledge and acknowledge the olfactory sensations emanating from the vessel prior to consuming the beverage. Take a deep breath and permit the aromatic fragrances to encompass your sensory perception.

- Consume the tea gradually, ensuring that each sip is savored and allowed to linger on the taste buds. It is advisable to observe and acknowledge the various flavors and sensations that manifest during the act of consuming tea, while also appreciating the contemplative nature inherent in this practice.

- Incorporate the practice of mindfulness while savoring your beverage of choice, such as the Spirit World Herbal Tea. Experience the calming effects of tea as it envelops your senses, connecting you to the present moment and cultivating a state of inner serenity.

The Spirit World Herbal Tea provides a tranquil and captivating encounter that reflects the ethereal domain of spiritual entities. By means of a combination of meticulously chosen botanicals, this infusion extends an invitation to partake in a voyage characterized by tranquility and self-reflection. The process entails collecting various herbs, making necessary preparations with a teapot, and anticipating the consumption of a cup of Spirit World Herbal Tea. This beverage offers an experience that transports individuals to a state of tranquility, facilitating a reconnection with the harmonious and serene atmosphere depicted in the Avatar universe.

CHAPTER 3

CONCLUSION OF AVATAR THE LAST AIRBENDER RECIPES

The Avatar: The Last Airbender Cookbook offers readers an immersive gastronomic journey into the rich and multifaceted universe of the acclaimed animated series. This cookbook offers an opportunity for fans and food enthusiasts to delve into the diverse culinary traditions of the four nations, including the bold and fiery flavors of the Fire Nation, the hearty and nourishing dishes of the Water Tribe, the wholesome cuisine of the Earth Kingdom, the light and simple treats of the Air Nomads, and the ethereal beverages of the Spirit World.

Throughout history, food has consistently held a prominent position within human culture, fulfilling various essential functions such as providing nourishment, facilitating communal festivities, and contributing to the formation of individual and collective identities. Within the realm of Avatar, the significance of food extends beyond its basic sustenance, assuming a profound role as a manifestation of the characters' personal growth and the rich cultural tapestry woven throughout the series. The Avatar: The Last Airbender Cookbook effectively encapsulates this essence by authentically recreating the flavors and aromas of the Avatar universe, thereby enabling readers to establish a tangible and sensory connection with the show.

This cookbook commemorates the significance of cultural diversity and the unifying potential of food by featuring recipes influenced by the Fire Nation, Water Tribe, Earth Kingdom, Air Nomads, and the

Spirit World. Every recipe provides insight into the culinary customs and principles of the corresponding countries, emphasizing the distinctive tastes and components that render them exceptional.

The culinary traditions of the Fire Nation exemplify the intrepid nature and resolute resolve of its populace. The culinary offerings of the Fire Nation, such as the spicy ramen, sizzling Fire Flakes, and other dishes with a fiery flavor profile, serve as a representation of the profound passion and intensity that characterizes the cultural essence of this nation. These recipes encourage readers to embrace robust flavors and cultivate their own culinary curiosity in the kitchen.

The culinary traditions of the Water Tribe pay homage to the unwavering determination and ingenuity demonstrated by its residents. The seafood stew, characterized by its robust and comforting qualities, serves as a tribute to the abundant resources of the ocean and the communal ethos that defines the Water Tribe. These recipes facilitate a connection between readers and the significance of community, family, and the nourishing properties of food.

The recipes of the Earth Kingdom exemplify a profound appreciation for the abundant diversity and profound connection to the natural environment. The cabbage rolls, characterized by their nutritious components and rustic taste, serve as a representation of the Earth Kingdom's agricultural prosperity and harmonious relationship with the natural environment. These recipes promote an appreciation for the aesthetic value of simplicity, the significance of sustainable practices, and the abundance of resources offered by the planet.

The culinary preparations of the Air Nomads effectively embody the essence of their lifestyle, characterized by its emphasis on lightness and simplicity. The fruit pies, characterized by their delicate and delightful nature, symbolize the Air Nomads' profound reverence for the bountiful offerings of the natural world and their commitment to maintaining a state of harmonious coexistence. The presented recipes serve as a source of inspiration for individuals to adopt a mindset of simplicity, mindfulness, and the appreciation of the inherent taste profiles found within fresh ingredients.

The recipes from the Spirit World provide a unique opportunity to gain insight into the intangible and enigmatic dimension that serves as a conduit between the realms of the Avatar universe. The herbal infusion, comprising a meticulously curated assortment of botanicals, elicits a profound state of serenity and self-reflection. The presented recipes encourage readers to delve into the spiritual dimension of food, facilitating a more profound connection with one's inner self and the surrounding environment.

When engaging with the Avatar: The Last Airbender Cookbook, readers are presented with the chance to not only replicate the delectable recipes but also establish a connection with the values and themes that the series encapsulates. By engaging in the process of culinary preparation and communal consumption of these dishes, individuals have the opportunity to wholeheartedly embrace a multitude of cultural traditions, expand their knowledge of unfamiliar ingredients, and commemorate the unifying force that food possesses in fostering social connections.

The Avatar: The Last Airbender Cookbook transcends its role as a mere compilation of culinary instructions, instead serving as an homage to the profound influence of the television series and its enduring resonance among a global community of enthusiasts. The text extends an invitation to readers to enter the realm of the Avatar universe, where they can fully engage with the sensory experiences of taste, smell, and narrative that contribute to its enthralling nature.

Whether one possesses an unwavering devotion to the series, harbors a fervent interest in gastronomy and its novel and captivating tastes, or merely seeks a means to establish a connection with the realm of Avatar, this culinary compendium serves as an ideal accompaniment. This proposition encourages individuals to adopt a mindset that values exploration and novelty, acknowledges the wide range of cultural expressions, and engages in the exploration of global perspectives by means of culinary experiences.

At this juncture, it is imperative to assemble the necessary ingredients, equip oneself with an apron, and commence an individual gastronomic expedition spanning the four nations and the Spirit World. May the kitchen be imbued with the fragrances characteristic of the Fire Nation, the palatable sensations associated with the Water Tribe, the earthly essence representative of the Earth Kingdom, the ethereal quality reminiscent of the Air Nomads, and the serene ambiance evocative of the Spirit World. Allow the Avatar: The Last Airbender Cookbook to serve as your authoritative reference as you craft indelible culinary experiences and establish a profound connection with the enchantment encapsulated within this adored television series.

THE END